Chefs' Special

Kashmiri Kitchen

Chefs' Special

Kashmiri Kitchen

Purnima Kachru

Lustre Press
Roli Books

Flavours of Kashmir

Each and every particle of my Kashmir is endowed with hospitality,
Even the rocks on the wayside offer me water to quench my thirst.
                                                    Sir Mohammed Iqbal

Kashmiri cooking tradition, influenced by the cuisines of the invaders from Central Asia amongst others, is today a harmonious fusion of several cultures. There are two types of Kashmiri cuisine: Pundit cuisine and the Muslim cuisine. This book features Pundit cuisine. Traditional Pundit cuisine is dominated by powdered and whole spices. In recent years, onions, tomatoes and garlic have also been included. Most of the cooking is done in mustard oil or *ghee* (clarified butter).

Unlike in most parts of India, the Kashmiri Brahmin is allowed to eat lamb, fish and duck. This book offers a wide selection of non-vegetarian and vegetarian preparations. *Yakhni*—a rich meat stock cooked in yoghurt, *Hak*—a leafy green vegetable boiled with very few spices, and boiled rice form a characteristic Kashmiri meal. *Roganjosh*—a meat preparation—is necessary to complete a typical Kashmiri spread. *Goshtaba* and *Rista*, delicacies for discerning palates, are gourmet preferences (but do not figure in this book on Pundit cuisine) from the Muslim table.

Though traditionally, chicken and eggs were considered unclean and, therefore, not cooked in the

Pundit kitchen, with the passage of time this belief has disappeared. Many lamb recipes are now cooked with chicken as a variation.

Food plays an important part in the rituals and customs of the Pundits. The most important festival celebrated by the Pundits is Herat or Shivratri. The family gathers together to supplicate Lord Shiva and feast in his honour. A sumptuous dinner usually includes *Roganjosh*, *Yakhni*, *Kalia*, *Kashur Gaad* and *Kofta*.

On Navreh, the first day of the Navratras and the beginning of the year according to the Vikrami Samvat (calendar), a variety of vegetarian dishes, especially *Hak*, and different dishes of *Chaman* (cottage cheese) are prepared. On Janamashtami people generally keep a fast and eat only fruits and fried potatoes with green chilli chutney and yoghurt.

On Yagnopavit, the sacred thread ceremony, *Dum Olu* and *Dal* (cooked in big clay ovens, over a low flame) are served with rice. Shishur is celebrated when a new bride or baby is welcomed into the family. It is believed that the celebrations of Shishur keeps evil spirits away. On this day all relatives are invited and served lamb *Kalia* and rice.

Kashmiri Pundit cuisine is not difficult to cook. Crisp, tangy, nutritious, delicious, spicy and wholesome - take 100 gm of adventurous spirit, deep fry in 10 tbsp of enthusiasm, season with a pinch of experimentation and create your own Kashmiri gourmet delight!

Kashmiri Spices and Condiments

Kashmiri Pundit cuisine uses both whole and ground spices. The most commonly used are:

Whole spices: Cloves (*laung*), cinnamon (*dalchini*), black cardamoms (*bari elaichi*), green cardamoms (*choti elaichi*), cumin seeds (*jeera*), caraway seeds (*kala/shahi jeera*), black pepper (*kali mirch*), bayleaves (*tej patta*) and saffron (*kesar*).

Asafoetida (*hing*): This can also be used and stored in liquid form. Mix 20 gm of asafoetida in 100 ml of water. Keep it in a bottle. Use 4-6 drops instead of a pinch of asafoetida.

Ground spices: Although most of these can now be bought, the traditional way of preparing them is listed below:

Turmeric (*haldi*) powder: Powder dry turmeric, sift through a fine sieve and store in an airtight jar.

Ginger powder (*saunth*): Grind dry ginger, sift through a fine sieve and then store in an airtight jar.

Aniseed (*saunf*) powder: Pick and clean whole aniseed, dry roast for a minute. Powder and then sift through a sieve and store in an airtight jar.

Red chilli (*lal mirch*) powder: Deseed dry red chillies. Oil and powder; sift and store in an airtight jar.

◀ *Clockwise from top: Red chilli powder, Coriander powder, Turmeric powder, Saffron, Green cardamoms, Ginger powder;* **centre:** *Cloves*

Garam masala powder: Prepare by grinding together the following spices: 200 gm cumin seeds (*jeera*), 10 gm cloves (*laung*), 10 gm nutmeg (*jaiphal*), 10 gm mace (*javitri*), 50 gm cinnamon (*dalchini*) sticks, 50 gm black cardamom seeds (*bari elaichi*), 5 gm black peppercorns (*kali mirch*) which is optional.

Sieve the spices and store in an airtight jar. Prepare the garam masala in small quantities, since it loses its aroma if kept for too long.

Spice cake (*tikki masala*): Take 100 gm asafoetida (*hing*), 100 gm black gram (*urad dal*) powder, 50 gm ginger powder (*saunth*), 100 gm red chilli powder, 50 gm aniseed (*saunf*) powder, 25 gm coriander (*dhaniya*) powder, 15 gm garam masala, 10 gm black cardamom (*bari elaichi*) powder, 10 gm cinnamon (*dalchini*) powder, 25 gm cumin seed (*jeera*) powder, 5 gm mace (*javitri*) powder, 5 gm nutmeg (*jaiphal*) powder, 10 gm cloves (*laung*) powder, 5 gm black cumin seed (*shahi jeera*) powder, 5 gm carom seeds (*ajwain*), 100 ml oil, 100 gm salt and 200 ml water.

Dissolve the asafoetida in ½ cup of water. Strain it into a big bowl. Add all the ingredients and the remaining water. Mix well and knead into a hard dough. Divide the dough into 20-25 equal portions and then shape each portion into round balls. Flatten each ball into round cakes. Place these on a greased tray and then sun-dry for one whole day. Turn over and dry the other side also for one whole day. When they are completely dry, store them in an airtight jar, and use as and when required.

Koftas
Mince rolls in curry

Preparation time: 20 min.
Cooking time: 25 min.
Serves: 4-6

Ingredients:

Lamb mince (*keema*), without fat,
    finely ground — 500 gm
Red chilli powder — 1½ tsp / 7½ gm
Ginger powder (*saunth*) — 1 tsp / 5 gm
Aniseed (*saunf*) powder — 3 tsp / 15 gm
Asafoetida (*hing*) — 2 pinches
Yoghurt (*dahi*) — 3 tbsp / 45 gm
Oil (for mince) — 2 tbsp / 30 ml
Black cardamom (*bari elaichi*)
    seeds; crushed, skins kept aside — 3
Whole Bengal gram (*bhuna channa*), roasted,
    powdered, (optional) — 2 tbsp / 30 gm
Salt to taste
Oil — 4 tbsp / 60 ml
Water — 1 cup / 200 ml

Garam masala — ½ tsp / 3 gm
Cloves (*laung*) — 4
Bayleaves (*tej patta*) — 2

Method:

1. Take the minced meat in a bowl, add red chilli powder, ginger powder (¼ tsp), aniseed powder (1 tsp), asafoetida (1 pinch), yoghurt (1 tbsp), oil (2 tbsp), black cardamom seeds, whole Bengal gram powder and half of the salt. Knead well with your hand till the spices are well blended and the mixture starts to grease your hands.

2. Make 15 equal portions of the mixture. On a flat greased surface, roll each portion gently into a 3"-long sausage or kofta. Put aside.

Lamb

9

3. Heat the oil in a deep pan. Mix together the red chilli powder and yoghurt. Add to the oil, stirring briskly. When the oil separates, add the water and stir again.

4. Add the remaining ginger powder, aniseed powder and garam masala powder, remaining asafoetida, cloves, bayleaves, black cardamom skins and the remaining salt into the pan. Cook till the gravy comes to a boil.

5. Carefully slide in the koftas, one at a time, and cook on a high flame till the gravy starts to thicken. Lower the flame and cook, stirring gently till the oil separates.

6. Serve hot. This recipe is best served with rice.

Longer Lasting!
Home ground masala powder will last longer if you add a teaspoon of vinegar to it before storing.

Buzith Mahts
Fried mince cutlets

Preparation time: 15 min.
Cooking time: 15 min.
Serves: 6 8

Ingredients:

Lamb mince	500 gm
Red chilli powder	½ tsp / 3 gm
Ginger powder (*saunth*)	½ tsp / 3 gm
Aniseed (*saunf*) powder	1 tsp / 5 gm
Garam masala (see p. 8)	½ tsp / 3 gm
Gram flour (*besan*) powder, roasted, (optional)	1 tbsp / 15 gm
Salt to taste	
Asafoetida (*hing*)	a pinch
Black cardamom (*bari elaichi*) seeds	1
Yoghurt (*dahi*)	1 tbsp / 15 gm
Oil	2 tbsp / 30 ml
Oil for frying	1 cup / 200 ml

Method:

1. Mix together all the ingredients except the oil for frying.
2. Knead with your hands till the mixture is well blended. Divide the mixture into 15-16 equal portions. Shape each portion into flat round cutlets. Put aside.
3. Heat the oil (for frying) in a pan. Shallow fry the cutlets a few at a time, on a high flame until golden brown on both sides.
4. Serve hot as a snack with tea or drinks.

Chokhta
Roasted lamb

Preparation time: 5 min.
Cooking time: 40 min.
Serves: **6-8**

Ingredients:

Lamb, cleaned and cut	1 kg
Water	1½ cups / 300 ml
Oil	½ cup / 100 ml
Salt to taste	
Asafoetida (*hing*)	2 pinches
Red chilli powder	2 tsp / 10 gm
Ginger powder (*saunth*)	1½ tsp / 8 gm

Method:

1. Put the lamb in a heavy-bottomed pot with the water, oil, salt and asafoetida. Cook covered, over a high flame for 20 minutes. Stir occasionally to ensure that it gets evenly done.
2. When the liquid dries and the oil surfaces, lower the flame and cook till it is deep brown in colour and a little crisp to touch, stirring continuously.
3. Add the red chilli powder mixed in a few spoons of water and stir briskly over a high flame till it becomes a rich red colour.
4. Add a few spoons of water and the ginger powder. Stir briskly, over a high flame, till the oil surfaces. Remove and serve accompanied by plain rice.

Note: *This is a spicy and pungent dish. Vary the quantity of red chilli powder and ginger powder to suit your taste.*

Lamb

Kabargah
Fried ribs

Preparation time: 10 min.
Cooking time: 45 min.
Serves: 4-6

Lamb

Ingredients:

Lamb ribs, 3" x 5" pieces	1 kg
Milk	2½ cups / 500 ml
Black cardamoms (*bari elaichi*), crushed	3
Cinnamon (*dalchini*) sticks	2
Cloves (*laung*)	4
Bayleaves (*tej patta*)	2
Garam masala (see p. 8)	1 tsp / 5 gm
Asafoetida (*hing*)	a pinch
Salt	2 tsp / 10 gm
Clarified butter (*ghee*)	1½ cups / 300 gm
Yoghurt (*dahi*)	½ cup / 100 gm
Red chilli powder	½ tsp / 3 gm
Silver leaves (*chandi vark*)	5-6

Method:

1. Put the ribs in a pot; add milk, black cardamoms, cinnamon sticks, cloves, bayleaves, garam masala, asafoetida and salt. Cook till the milk gets absorbed.
2. Remove from the flame, and transfer the ribs to a large plate. Keep aside.
3. Heat the clarified butter. Meanwhile, whisk together the yoghurt, red chilli powder and a little salt until smooth in consistency.
4. Dip each rib into the yoghurt and fry to a rich brown colour. Drain excess oil and transfer to a serving dish.
5. Garnish with silver leaves and serve hot, as a snack or as part of the main course.

Tsok-Tsarvan
Tangy liver curry

Preparation time: 10 min.
Cooking time: 20 min.
Serves: 4-6

Ingredients:

Liver, cut into 1 cm pieces	500 gm
Oil	4 tbsp / 60 gm
Asafoetida (*hing*)	a pinch
Salt to taste	
Cloves (*laung*)	2
Red chilli powder	1 tsp / 5 gm
Aniseed (*saunf*) powder	2 tsp / 10 gm
Water	1 cup / 200 ml
Ginger powder (*saunth*)	½ tsp / 3 gm
Garam masala (see p. 8)	½ tsp / 3 gm
Tamarind (*imli*), extract	¼ cup / 50 gm
Green chillies, slit	2

Method:

1. Heat the oil in a pan. Add the liver, asafoetida, salt and cloves to it. Sauté for 4-5 minutes over a low flame.
2. Mix the red chilli powder in a little water and add to the liver. Stir briskly over a high flame for a few seconds.
3. Add the water, aniseed powder, ginger powder and garam masala powder. Cook till the water is reduced to half.
4. Add the tamarind extract and green chillies. Cook till the oil surfaces. Remove from the flame and serve with bread or rice.

Tsarvan Olu
Curried liver and potatoes

Preparation time: 10 min.
Cooking time: 20 min.
Serves: 4-6

Ingredients:

Liver, cut into 1" cubes	500 gm
Oil	4 tbsp / 60 ml
Potatoes, peeled, cut into 1" cubes	1¼ cups / 250 gm
Tomatoes, finely chopped	½ cup / 100 gm
Cloves (*laung*)	4
Asafoetida (*hing*)	a pinch
Salt to taste	
Red chilli powder	1 tsp / 5 gm
Water	1½ cups / 300 ml
Ginger powder (*saunth*)	1 tsp / 5 gm
Aniseed (*saunf*) powder	2 tsp / 10 gm
Green chillies	2

Method:

1. Heat the oil in a heavy-bottomed pot. Add the liver, potatoes, tomatoes, cloves, asafoetida and salt into the pot. Cook, stirring occasionally, till the liquid dries and the oil separates.
2. Mix the red chilli powder in a little water and add to the liver. Stir for a few seconds, then add the remaining water and bring to a boil.
3. Put in the ginger powder, aniseed powder and green chillies. Cook till the gravy thickens a little. Serve hot.

Lamb

Syun Methi
Lamb cooked with fenugreek

Preparation time: 15 min.
Cooking time: 30 min.
Serves: 4-6

Ingredients:

Lamb, washed, cut into 2" pieces	1 kg
Water	2 cups / 400 ml
Salt to taste	
Turmeric (*haldi*) powder	1 tsp / 10 gm
Aniseed (*saunf*) powder	2 tsp / 10 gm
Ginger powder (*saunth*)	2 tsp / 10 gm
Cloves (*laung*)	3
Cinnamon (*dalchini*), 2" stick	1
Bayleaves (*tej patta*)	a few
Black cardamoms (*bari elaichi*)	3
Garam masala (see p. 8)	1 tsp / 5 gm
Asafoetida (*hing*)	a pinch
Fenugreek (*methi*) leaves	2½ cups / 500 gm
Clarified butter (*ghee*)	8 tbsp / 120 gm
Green chillies	3

Method:

1. Put the lamb into a deep pot/pressure cooker, with the water, salt, turmeric powder, aniseed powder, ginger powder, cloves, cinnamon stick, bayleaves, black cardamoms, garam masala and asafoetida.
2. Cook over a high flame for 15 minutes (4 whistles in a pressure cooker), till the lamb is almost done. Take out the pieces from the stock and put aside.
3. Clean, wash and boil the fenugreek leaves. Strain and grind them to a paste.
4. Heat the oil in a deep pan; add the fenugreek to it and sauté for 5 minutes, stirring frequently.
5. Add the lamb and sauté for 5 minutes. Add the stock and cook till the lamb gets done. Remove from fire, garnish with green chillies and serve.

Yakhni
Stewed lamb in yoghurt

Preparation time: 10 min.
Cooking time: 30 min.
Serves: 4-6

Lamb

Ingredients:

Lamb, washed, cut into 2" pieces	1 kg
Ginger powder (*saunth*)	2 tsp / 10 gm
Aniseed (*saunf*) powder	4 tsp / 20 gm
Garam masala (see p. 8)	1 tsp / 5 gm
Asafoetida (*hing*)	a pinch
Black cardamoms (*bari elaichi*), crushed	3
Cloves (*laung*)	4-5
Bayleaves (*tej patta*)	2-3
Salt to taste	
Yoghurt (*dahi*), whisked	2 cups/ 400 gm
Clarified butter (*ghee*)	4 tsp / 20 gm
Green cardamoms (*choti elaichi*), crushed	4
Water	2 cups / 400 ml

Method:

1. Put the lamb into a deep pot or a pressure cooker with water. Add ginger powder, aniseed powder, garam masala, asafoetida, black cardamoms, 2 cloves, bayleaves and salt. Cook for 15 minutes, or till it is almost done.

2. Add yoghurt, stirring till it comes to a boil. Lower the flame and simmer till the gravy thickens and the lamb becomes tender. Remove from the flame.

3. Heat the clarified butter in a small pan; add the remaining cloves and green cardamoms to it. Sauté for a few seconds and then add to the cooked lamb. Serve, accompanied with steaming hot rice.

Kalia
Lamb stew

Preparation time: 10 min.
Cooking time: 30 min
Serves: 6-8

Ingredients:

Lamb	1 kg
Water	1½ cups / 300 ml
Turmeric (*haldi*) powder	1 tsp / 5 gm
Ginger powder (*saunth*)	1 tsp / 5 gm
Aniseed (*saunf*) powder	3 tsp / 15 gm
Salt to taste	
Asafoetida (*hing*)	a pinch
Black cardamoms (*bari elaichi*), crushed	2
Bayleaves (*tej patta*)	2
Milk	¼ cup / 50 ml
Yoghurt (*dahi*)	¼ tsp / 50 ml
Oil (for tempering)	2 tbsp / 30 ml
Garam masala (see p. 8)	½ tsp / 3 gm
Cloves (*laung*)	4
Green cardamoms (*choti elaichi*)	4

Method:

1. Cook the lamb with water in a pot, on high flame.
2. Add the turmeric, ginger and aniseed powders, salt, asafoetida, black cardamoms and bayleaves. Cook covered, for about 20 minutes on a high flame. Stir occasionally.
3. Once the lamb is almost tender, cook uncovered over a low flame.
4. Beat the milk and yoghurt into a smooth mixture. Add this to the lamb, stirring constantly. Bring to a boil over a high flame, stirring continuously. Cook for 5 minutes, after it comes to a boil.
5. In a small pan, heat the oil. Sauté the cloves and green cardamoms for a few seconds. Add this spice mixture to the lamb. Serve with steamed rice.

Roganjosh
Lamb curry

Preparation time: 10 min.
Cooking time: 35 min.
Serves: 4-6

Lamb

Ingredients:

Lamb, washed well	1 kg
Yoghurt (*dahi*), whisked	1 cup / 200 gm
Cloves (*laung*)	4
Cinnamon (*dalchini*), 2" stick	1
Black cardamoms (*bari elaichi*)	3
Bayleaves (*tej patta*)	2
Clarified butter (*ghee*)	¾ cup / 150 gm
Salt to taste	
Asafoetida (*hing*)	a pinch
Red chilli powder	2 tsp / 10 gm
Water	2 cups / 400 ml
Ginger powder (*saunth*)	2 tsp / 10 gm
Aniseed (*saunf*) powder	4 tsp / 20 gm
Saffron (*kesar*), (optional)	½ tsp / 3 gm
Garam masala (see p. 8)	1 tsp / 5 gm

Method:

1. Marinate the lamb in yoghurt, cloves, cinnamon, black cardamoms and bayleaves for 10 minutes.
2. Heat oil in a deep pan. Add the lamb and cover till it stops spattering. Add salt and asafoetida and stir.
3. Cook over high flame till the yoghurt dries. Lower the flame and stir briskly to prevent from sticking.
4. Sprinkle a little water and stir till the meat browns. Repeat this twice, cooking till the oil separates.
5. Add the red chilli powder mixed with a little water. Cook over high flame, stirring briskly. Add water, ginger and aniseed powders; cook for 15 minutes.
6. Soak the saffron in 4 tsp of hot water; grind and add to the lamb. Cook until the lamb is tender and the oil separates. Sprinkle garam masala and serve hot.

Kokur Nadur
Chicken with lotus stems

Preparation time: 15 min.
Cooking time: 40 min.
Serves: 4-6

Ingredients:

Chicken (broiler), washed, cut into 8 pieces	1 kg
Lotus stems (*bhein*), medium	1 kg
Oil for frying	1 cup / 200 ml
Oil	4 tbsp / 60 ml
Red chilli powder	1½ tsp / 8 gm
Water	1½ cups / 300 ml
Ginger powder (*saunth*)	1 tsp / 5 gm
Aniseed (*saunf*) powder	3 tsp / 15 gm
Salt to taste	
Asafoetida (*hing*)	a pinch
Cloves (*laung*)	4
Black cardamoms (*bari elaichi*), crushed	2
Bayleaves (*tej patta*)	2
Tikki masala, crushed (see p. 8)	½ tsp / 3 gm

Method:

1. Wash, peel and cut the lotus stems into 2"-cylindrical pieces. Wash well to remove all the traces of mud. Put aside to drain.

2. Heat oil in a deep pan. Fry the chicken to a golden brown and put aside. Fry the lotus stems in the same oil till golden brown and keep aside.

3. Heat 4 tbsp of oil in a heavy-bottomed pan. Add red chilli powder mixed in a little water. Stir for a few seconds, add water and bring to a boil.

4. Add the chicken, lotus stems and all the remaining ingredients except *tikki masala*. Cook for 10-15 minutes on high flame. When the gravy thickens, add *tikki masala* and cook further for 1-2 minutes, stirring gently. Serve hot.

Chicken

Kokur Roganjosh

Chicken curry

Preparation time: 10 min.
Cooking time: 20 min.
Serves: 4-6

Ingredients:

Chicken (broiler), cut into 8-10 pieces	1 kg
Yoghurt (*dahi*)	1 cup / 200 gm
Salt to taste	
Black cardamoms (*bari elaichi*), crushed	2
Oil	4 tbsp / 60 ml
Asafoetida (*hing*)	a pinch
Bayleaves (*tej patta*)	2
Cinnamon (*dalchini*) sticks	2
Cloves (*laung*)	3
Red chilli powder	1 tsp / 5 gm
Water	1 cup / 200 ml
Ginger powder (*saunth*)	1 tsp / 5 gm
Aniseed (*saunf*) powder	3 tsp / 15 gm
Garam masala (see p. 8)	1 tsp / 5 gm

Method:

1. Marinate the chicken with yoghurt, salt and black cardamoms. Refrigerate for 2-3 hours.
2. Heat the oil in a heavy-bottomed pot. Add the chicken, asafoetida, bayleaves, cinnamon and cloves. Cook till the yoghurt dries and the oil surfaces (about 10 minutes), stirring gently. Lower the flame and cook, turning frequently, till the chicken becomes a rich brown colour.
3. Mix the red chilli powder with a few spoons of water and add it into the pot. Stir briskly for a few seconds over a high flame. Add 1 cup of water, ginger, aniseed and garam masala powders. Cook till the gravy thickens and the oil surfaces.
4. Serve hot with rice.

Chicken

Kashur Gaad
Tamarind-flavoured fish curry

Preparation time: 10 min.
Cooking time: 35 min.
Serves: 6-8

Ingredients:

Fish fillets, washed, drained	1 kg
Oil	2 cups / 400 ml
Cloves (*laung*)	4
Black cardamoms (*bari elaichi*), crushed	2
Red chilli powder	2 tsp / 10 gm
Water	2 cups / 400 ml
Ginger powder (*saunth*)	1½ tsp / 8 gm
Aniseed (*saunf*) powder	3 tsp / 15 gm
Garam masala (see p. 8)	1 tsp / 5 gm
Asafoetida (*hing*)	a pinch
Salt to taste	
Tamarind (*imli*), extract	4 tbsp / 60 gm
Green chillies, slit	3
Tikki masala (see p. 8)	1 tsp / 5 gm

(Photograph on page 2)

Method:

1. Heat the oil in a big pan. Fry the fish over a high flame, till crisp and golden brown on both sides. Drain excess oil and keep aside.

2. In a heavy-bottomed pan, reheat ½ cup oil. Add the cloves and black cardamoms, sauté for a few seconds. Add red chilli powder mixed with 4 tsp of water and stir briskly till the oil reddens.

3. Add water, ginger powder, aniseed powder, garam masala, asafoetida and salt. Bring to a boil. Gently add the fish and cook till the gravy thickens.

4. Add tamarind extract and green chillies. Stir carefully. Add the *tikki masala*, cook for a few more minutes till the oil separates. Serve with plain rice.

Muji Gaad
Fish à la radish

Preparation time: 15 min.
Cooking time: 40 min.
Serves: 6-8

Ingredients:

Fish fillets, washed, drained	1 kg
Radish (*mooli*), peeled, washed	250 gm
Tomatoes, grated	1 cup / 200 gm
Oil	2 cups / 400 ml
Cloves (*laung*)	4
Red chilli powder	2 tsp / 10 gm
Water	2 cups / 400 ml
Ginger powder (*saunth*)	1½ tsp / 8 gm
Aniseed (*saunf*) powder	3 tsp / 15 gm
Garam masala (see p. 8)	1 tsp / 5 gm
Asafoetida (*hing*)	a pinch
Black cardamoms (*bari elaichi*), crushed	2
Green chillies, slit	3
Salt to taste	
Tikki masala (see p. 8), crushed	1 tsp / 5 gm

Method:

1. Cut the radish into 3"- long pieces and then halve each piece. Put aside.
2. Heat 1½ cups oil in a big pan. Fry the fillets over a high flame, until crisp and golden brown on both sides. Drain oil and put aside. Deep fry the radish in the same oil, till golden brown and put aside
3. Heat remaining oil, add the cloves and red chilli powder mixed with water. Stir briskly for a few seconds, add tomatoes. Cook until the oil separates.
4. Add water, ginger powder, aniseed powder, garam masala, asafoetida, black cardamoms, green chillies and salt. Stir well and then add the fish fillets. Cook for about 10-15 minutes, till gravy thickens.
5. Sprinkle *tikki masala*, cook for a minute. Serve hot.

Thool Zamboor

Fried egg curry

Preparation time: 15 min.
Cooking time: 40 min.
Serves: 2-4

Ingredients:

Eggs, hard-boiled, shelled	8
Oil for frying	½ cup / 100 ml
Tomato purée	1¼ cups / 150 gm
Oil	3 tbsp / 45 ml
Red chilli powder	1 tsp / 5 gm
Salt to taste	
Cloves (*laung*)	2
Black cardamoms (*bari elaichi*), crushed	2
Bayleaves (*tej patta*)	2
Asafoetida (*hing*)	a pinch
Water	1½ cups / 300 ml
Ginger powder (*saunth*)	1 tsp / 5 gm
Aniseed (*saunf*) powder	2 tsp / 10 gm
Garam masala (see p. 8)	½ tsp / 3 gm

Method:

1. Pierce the eggs with a needle or a toothpick right through, 4-5 times.
2. Heat the oil (for frying); fry the eggs to a golden brown. Remove and keep aside.
3. Heat the 3 tbsp oil in a pot. Add the red chilli powder mixed in a little water and stir briskly for a few seconds. Add the purée, salt, cloves, black cardamoms, bayleaves and asafoetida. Cook till the oil separates.
4. Add water, eggs, ginger and aniseed powders. Cook over a high flame till the gravy thickens. Stir frequently to ensure nothing sticks to the bottom of the pot. Sprinkle the garam masala powder and serve hot.

Eggs

Olu Manjivor
Potato cutlets

Preparation time: 10 min.
Cooking time: 10 min.
Serves: 4-6

Vegetarian

Ingredients:

Potatoes, peeled, washed, grated   250 gm
Arrowroot (*araroht*)   2 tbsp / 30 gm
Salt to taste
Ginger (*adrak*), grated   2 tbsp / 30 gm
Red chilli powder (optional)   ½ tsp / 3 gm
Oil   ½ cup / 100 ml

Method:

1. In a bowl, mix together the potatoes, the arrowroot, salt, ginger and red chilli powder.
2. Divide the mixture into six equal portions. Roll and shape each portion into flat rounds (like cutlets).
3. Heat the oil in a shallow pan. Carefully fry the cutlets a few at a time, until they are golden brown on both sides. Serve hot.

Dum Olu
Fried potato curry

Preparation time: 10 min.
Cooking time: 40 min.
Serves: 4-6

Vegetarian

Ingredients:

Potatoes, boiled, soaked in cold water	750 gm
Oil for frying	1 cup / 200 ml
Oil	5 tbsp / 75 ml
Yoghurt (*dahi*)	4 tbsp / 60 gm
Red chilli powder	2 tsp / 10 gm
Water	1 cup / 200 ml
Aniseed (*saunf*) powder	1 tbsp / 15 gm
Ginger powder (*saunth*)	1½ tsp / 8 gm
Garam masala (see p. 8)	1 tsp / 5 gm
Asafoetida (*hing*)	a pinch
Black cardamoms (*bari elaichi*)	2
Bayleaves (*tej patta*)	2
Cloves (*laung*)	4
Salt to taste	

Method:

1. Peel the potatoes and pierce right through with a toothpick, making 3-4 punctures through each.
2. Heat the oil and fry the potatoes, till they are golden brown. Drain excess oil and put aside.
3. Heat the oil (5 tbsp) in a heavy-bottomed pan. Mix together the yoghurt and red chilli powder and add to the pan. Stir briskly till it takes a nice red colour, without letting it stick to the bottom.
4. Add water, stir well and then add all the spices. Bring to a boil. Add the fried potatoes and cook over a low flame for 15 minutes.
5. Stir occasionally to prevent it from sticking to the bottom. Cook until the liquid is almost dry and the oil separates. Remove from flame and serve hot.

Paalak Olu
Spinach with potatoes

Preparation time: 15 min.
Cooking time: 30 min.
Serves: 4-6

Vegetarian

Ingredients:

Spinach (*palak*)	750 gm
Water for boiling	
Oil	4 tbsp / 60 ml
Cloves (*laung*)	3
Potatoes, peeled, washed, cut into 8 pieces	250 gm
Asafoetida (*hing*)	a pinch
Salt to taste	
Red chilli powder	1 tsp / 5 gm
Water	1½ cups / 300 ml
Ginger powder (*saunth*)	½ tsp / 3 gm
Turmeric (*haldi*) powder	½ tsp / 3 gm
Tikki masala, crushed (see p. 8)	½ tsp / 3 gm
Green chillies, slit	2

Method:

1. Remove the spinach stems and wash well.
2. Boil the spinach. After a few boils, drain the water and grind the spinach. Keep it aside.
3. In a deep pan, heat the oil. Sauté the cloves and potatoes for 1 minute. Add the spinach, asafoetida and salt. Cook till the liquid dries and the oil separates.
4. Mix the red chilli powder in a few spoons of water and add to the spinach. Stir briskly and add the water, ginger powder and turmeric powder. Cook till the water is almost dry.
5. Sprinkle the *tikki masala* and green chillies; cook further for 2-3 minutes. Serve hot with rice.

Tamatar Gogji
Turnips in tomato curry

Preparation time: 15 min.
Cooking time: 25 min.
Serves: 6-8

Ingredients:

Turnips (*shalgam*), medium	1 kg
Oil	3 tbsp / 45 ml
Garlic (*lasan*) paste	1 tsp / 5 gm
Asafoetida (*hing*)	a pinch
Cloves (*laung*)	4 tbsp / 60 gm
Black cardamons (*bari elaichi*)	2
Salt to taste	
Tomato purée	1¼ cups / 250 gm
Red chilli powder	½ tbsp / 8 gm
Water	1 cup / 200 ml
Ginger powder (*saunth*)	2 tsp / 10 gm
Aniseed (*saunf*) powder	1 tbsp / 15 gm
Tikki masala, crushed (see p. 8)	½ tsp / 3 gm

Method:

1. Remove the ends of the turnips. Cut the rest into 4 portions. Wash and put aside.
2. Heat the oil in a pot; add the garlic paste and asafoetida. Cook a little then add the cloves, black cardamoms, salt and turnips. Sauté for about 5 minutes on a low flame, stirring occasionally.
3. Add the tomato purée and cook till the oil separates. Mix the red chilli powder with a few tsp of water and add to the turnips. Stir well till it attains a nice red colour.
4. Quickly add the water, followed by ginger and aniseed powders. Cook till the turnips become tender. Sprinkle *tikki masala* and cook for 2 minutes. Serve hot with rice.

Tamatar Paneer

Cottage cheese in tomato sauce

Preparation time: 10 min.
Cooking time: 20-25 min.
Serves: 4-6

Vegetarian

Ingredients:

Cottage cheese (*paneer*), ½" thick pieces 500 gm
Oil for deep frying   1¼ cups / 250 ml
Water   1½ cups / 300 ml
Cloves (*laung*)   3
Black cardamoms (*bari elaichi*), crushed   2
Cinnamon (*dalchini*), 2" sticks   1
Bayleaves (*tej patta*)   2
Asafoetida (*hing*)   a pinch
Red chilli powder   1 tsp / 5 gm
Ginger powder (*saunth*)   1 tsp / 5 gm
Aniseed (*saunf*) powder   3 tsp / 15 gm
Garam masala (see p. 8)   1 tsp / 5 gm
Tomato purée   1¼ cups / 250 gm
Green chillies, sliced and salt to taste

(Photograph on front cover)

Method:

1. Heat the oil in a deep pan. Fry the cottage cheese until golden on the edges but not brown. Remove from the oil and soak in a pan of water.

2. Take a deep pot, reheat 4 tbsp oil. Add the cloves, black cardamoms, cinnamon sticks, bayleaves and asafoetida. Lower the flame and add the red chilli powder mixed with 4 tsp of water.

3. Stir briskly over high flame for 30 seconds. Gently add the cottage cheese (with water), ginger and aniseed powders, garam masala and salt. Cook for 10 minutes. Add the tomato purée, cook for 5-10 minutes, stirring carefully until the oil separates; remove from the fire.

4. Garnish with green chillies and serve with rice.

Dum Gogji
Curried turnips

Preparation time: 10 min.
Cooking time: 30 min.
Serves: 8-10

Ingredients:

Turnips (*shalgam*), washed	1 kg
Oil for frying	1 cup / 200 ml
Oil	4 tbsp / 60 ml
Cloves (*laung*)	5-6
Bayleaves (*tej patta*)	2
Black cardamoms (*bari elaichi*)	2
Salt to taste	
Asafoetida (*hing*)	a pinch
Red chilli powder	2 tsp / 10 gm
Yoghurt (*dahi*)	2 tbsp / 30 gm
Water	1 cup / 200 ml
Ginger powder (*saunth*)	1 tsp / 5 gm
Aniseed (*saunf*) powder	1 tbsp / 15 gm
Garam masala (see p. 8)	1 tsp / 5 gm
Cinnamon (*dalchini*), 2" stick	1

Method:

1. Remove the ends of the turnips and cut into ½"-thick rounds. Pierce with a fork and put aside.
2. Heat the oil (for frying) and fry the turnips to a golden brown. Put aside.
3. Heat 4 tbsp of oil. Add the cloves, bayleaves, black cardamoms, salt and asafoetida. Lower the flame.
4. Add the red chilli powder mixed in yoghurt. Stir briskly till the oil separates, ensuring that it does not stick to the bottom.
5. Stir in the water. Add the turnips, ginger and aniseed powders and garam masala. Cook for 10 minutes over high flame until the gravy thickens and the oil separates, stirring gently occasionally. Serve hot.

Chaman Olu

Cottage cheese and potatoes

Preparation time: 15 min.
Cooking time: 20 min.
Serves: 4-6

Vegetarian

Ingredients:

Cottage cheese (*paneer*)	500 gm
Potatoes, peeled, ½" thick rounds	150 gm
Oil for frying	1 cup / 200 ml
Water	1½ cups / 300 ml
Turmeric (*haldi*) powder	1 tsp / 5 gm
Ginger powder (*saunth*)	1 tsp / 5 gm
Aniseed (*saunf*) powder	2 tsp / 10 gm
Asafoetida (*hing*)	a pinch
Salt to taste	
Black cardamoms (*bari elaichi*), crushed	2
Yoghurt (*dahi*)	3 tbsp / 45 gm
Milk	3 tbsp / 45 ml
Clarified butter (*ghee*)	2 tbsp / 30 gm
Cloves (*laung*), crushed	3
Green cardamoms (*choti elaichi*), crushed	3
Green chillies, sliced	2

Method:

1. Cut the cottage cheese into 1½ x 2"x ½" pieces.
2. Heat the oil and fry the cottage cheese until it becomes golden at the edges. Transfer to a pot with water. Fry the potatoes and put them aside.
3. Put the pot with the cottage cheese and water over a high flame. Add turmeric, ginger and aniseed powders, asafoetida, salt, black cardamoms and potatoes. Cook until the gravy is reduced to half. Add the yoghurt and milk (whisked together). Bring to a boil, stirring constantly for 5 minutes; then remove from the flame.
4. In a pan, heat the clarified butter and sauté the cloves and green cardamoms. Add to the preparation; garnish with green chillies and serve.

Monji Kalia
Kohlrabi stew

Preparation time: 10 min.
Cooking time: 30 min.
Serves: 4-6

Ingredients:

Kohlrabi (*ganth gobhi*)	1 kg
Oil	1¼ cups / 250 ml
Cloves (*laung*)	4
Black cardamoms (*bari elaichi*), crushed	2
Asafoetida (*hing*)	a pinch
Water	1 cup / 200 ml
Turmeric (*haldi*) powder	1 tsp / 5 gm
Ginger powder (*saunth*)	1 tsp / 5 gm
Aniseed (*saunf*) powder	1 tbsp / 15 gm
Garam masala (see p. 8)	½ tsp / 3 gm
Salt to taste	
Milk	2 tbsp / 30 ml
Yoghurt (*dahi*)	2 tbsp / 30 gm
Green cardamoms (*choti elaichi*)	3

Method:

1. Wash, peel and cut the kohlrabi into 1" cubes.
2. Heat oil and fry the kohlrabi until golden. Drain and put aside.
3. Heat 3 tbsp oil in a deep pot; add the cloves, black cardamoms and asafoetida. Fry a little and then add the water. Cover to prevent the oil from spattering.
4. Add the kohlrabi, turmeric, ginger and aniseed powders, garam masala and salt. Cook over a high flame for 10 minutes.
5. Add the milk and yoghurt (whisked together), stirring constantly till it comes to a boil. Cook for 5 minutes and then remove from the flame.
6. Heat 1 tbsp of oil in a small pan; sauté the cardamoms and add this to the pot. Serve hot.

Nadur Monji
Lotus stem fingers

Preparation time: 15 min.
Cooking time: 15 min.
Serves: 6-8

Ingredients:

Lotus stems (*bhein*)	500 gm
Flour (*maida*)	½ cup / 100 gm
Soda-bi-carb	a pinch
Red chilli powder	1 tsp / 5 gm
Salt to taste	
Water	½ cup / 100 ml
Red colour (optional)	3-4 drops
Oil for frying	1 cup / 200 ml

Method:

1. Scrape the lotus stems and cut off the ends. Wash thoroughly under running water, ensuring that no mud remains in the stems.
2. Cut the stems into 3" pieces and then slice each piece into 4-6 fingers. Wash well again.
3. In a big bowl, mix flour, soda-bi-carb, red chilli powder, salt and enough water to make a batter of dropping consistency. Add the red colour.
4. Heat the oil in a deep pan. Dip each lotus stem piece into the batter and then deep fry until golden in colour.
5. Drain the excess oil and serve hot as a snack or as an accompaniment.

Nadur Yakhin
Lotus stems in yoghurt

Preparation time: 10 min.
Cooking time: 25 min.
Serves: 4-6

Ingredients:

Lotus stems (*bhein*)	½ kg
Water	2 cups / 400 ml
Aniseed (*saunf*) powder	1 tbsp / 15 gm
Ginger powder (*saunth*)	1 tsp / 5 gm
Black cardamoms (*bari elaichi*), lightly crushed	2
Bayleaves (*tej patta*)	2
Black peppercorns (*sabut kali mirch*)	4
Black cumin seeds (*shahi jeera*)	½ tsp / 3 gm
Asafoetida (*hing*)	a pinch
Salt to taste	
Yoghurt (*dahi*)	1¼ cups / 250 gm
Garam masala (see p. 8)	½ tsp / 3 gm
Oil	2 tbsp / 30 ml
Cloves (*laung*)	4
Green cardamoms (*choti elaichi*), crushed	4

Method:

1. Scrape the lotus stems. Cut into 2" cylindrical pieces. Wash well to remove all traces of mud.
2. To the water, add lotus stems, aniseed and ginger powders, black cardamoms, bayleaves, black cumin seeds, peppercorns, asafoetida and salt. Bring to a boil; cook for 15 minutes on high flame.
3. Whisk the yoghurt and the garam masala until smooth. Add to the pot. Cook for 5 minutes on high flame, till the gravy thickens and then leave the mixture to simmer.
4. In a another pan, heat the oil and sauté the cloves and green cardamoms. Add to the pot and cook for a few more minutes. Serve hot with boiled rice.

Nadur Roganjosh
Lotusroot roganjosh

Preparation time: 10 min.
Cooking time: 30 min.
Serves: 2-4

Ingredients:

Lotus root (*bhein*), scraped	500 gm
Oil	5 tbsp / 75 ml
Cumin seeds (*jeera*)	½ tsp / 3 gm
Cloves (*laung*)	3
Bayleaves (*tej patta*)	2
Black cardamoms (*bari elaichi*), crushed	2
Salt to taste	
Asafoetida (*hing*)	a pinch
Red chilli powder	1 tsp / 5 gm
Yoghurt (*dahi*)	2 tbsp / 30 gm
Water	1½ cups / 300 ml
Ginger powder (*saunth*)	1 tsp / 5 gm
Aniseed powder (*saunf*)	2 tsp / 10 gm
Garam masala (see p. 8)	½ tsp / 3 gm

Method:

1. Cut the lotus root into 2"-long pieces, and then further into halves. Wash well.

2. Heat the oil in a heavy-bottomed pan. Add the cumin seeds, cloves, bayleaves and black cardamons. Stir till they crackle.

3. Add the lotus root pieces, salt and asafoetida. Sauté over low heat for about 7 minutes, stirring to make sure that it does not stick to the bottom.

4. Mix the red chilli powder with the yoghurt and add. Stir vigorously for 30 seconds over a high flame. Mix in water.

5. Bring to a boil, add the ginger and aniseed powders and the garam masala. Cook for 10-15 minutes or till the water dries. Serve hot.

Phoolgobhi Roganjosh

Cauliflower curry

Preparation time: 15 min.
Cooking time: 40 min.
Serves: 1-6

Vegetarian

Ingredients:

Cauliflower (*phool gobi*)	1 kg
Oil for frying	1 cup / 200 ml
Oil	5 tbsp / 75 ml
Cloves (*laung*)	4
Bayleaves (*tej patta*)	2
Black cardamoms (*bari elaichi*), crushed	3
Asafoetida (*hing*)	a pinch
Red chilli powder	2 tsp / 10 gm
Yoghurt (*dahi*)	2 tbsp / 30 gm
Water	¾ cup / 150 ml
Salt to taste	
Ginger powder (*saunth*)	½ tbsp / 8 gm
Aniseed (*saunf*) powder	2 tsp / 10 gm
Garam masala (see p. 8)	1 tsp / 5 gm

Method:

1. Cut the cauliflower into 6-7 florets each. Soak in saline water for 3-4 minutes. Rinse and put aside.
2. Heat oil (for frying) in a deep pan. Fry the florets to a golden brown. Drain excess oil.
3. Heat 5 tbsp oil; add the cloves, bayleaves, black cardamoms and asafoetida. Stir over a low flame for a few seconds. Mix the red chilli powder with the yoghurt and add to the pan. Cook over a high flame till the oil separates, stirring continuously.
4. Add the water and stir. Add the cauliflower, salt, ginger and aniseed powders and garam masala. Cook for 10 minutes over a low flame, taking care that the mixture does not stick to the bottom.
5. Remove from the flame and serve hot.

Tsok Vangun
Tangy brinjals

Preparation time: 10 min.
Cooking time: 30 min.
Serves: 4-6

Vegetarian

Ingredients:

Brinjals (*baingan*), small	500 gm
Oil for frying	1 cup / 200 ml
Oil	3 tbsp / 45 ml
Red chilli powder	1 tsp / 5 gm
Water	1 cup / 200 ml
Ginger powder (*saunth*)	1 tsp / 5 gm
Aniseed (*saunf*) powder	2 tsp / 10 gm
Asafoetida (*hing*)	a pinch
Salt to taste	
Tamarind (*imli*) paste	4 tsp / 20 gm
Green chillies, slit	2

Method:

1. Snip the tips and tails of the brinjals and quarter them lengthwise. Soak in water until they are to be used, to prevent from turning brown.
2. Heat the oil (for frying) in a broad pan. Fry the brinjals to a golden brown. Remove from the oil and keep aside.
3. Heat 3 tbsp oil in a pan. Add red chilli powder, mixed with 4 tsp of water and stir. Add water, brinjals, ginger and aniseed powders, asafoetida and salt. Cook for 5 minutes on a high flame.
4. Mix in the tamarind paste, add the green chillies and cook till the gravy thickens and the oil separates. Serve hot.

Hak
Stir-fried spinach

Preparation time: 10 min.
Cooking time: 20 min.
Serves: 4 6

Vegetarian

Ingredients:

Spinach (*palak*)	1 kg
Mustard (*sarson*) oil	3 tbsp / 45 ml
Asafoetida (*hing*)	1 pinch
Salt to taste	
Whole red chillies (*sabut lal mirch*)	4
Water	2 cups / 400 ml
Sugar	a pinch
Tikki masala (see p. 8), crushed	¼ tsp

Method:

1. Clean and wash the spinach; keep aside.
2. Heat the oil in a pot; add the asafoetida, salt, whole red chillies and water. Cover immediately and wait till the oil stops spattering. Uncover and bring to a boil.
3. Add the spinach followed by sugar and stir well. Cook over a high flame for 15 minutes.
4. Add the *tikki masala* and cook for 5 minutes, stirring continuously.
5. Serve hot accompanied by steaming rice.

Dum Monji
Fried kohlrabi curry

Preparation time: 15 min.
Cooking time: 30 min
Serves: 4-6

Ingredients:

Kohlrabi (*ganth gobhi*)	1 kg
Oil for frying	1 cup / 200 ml
Oil	4 tbsp / 60 ml
Cloves (*laung*)	3-4
Bayleaves (*tej patta*)	2
Black cardamoms (*bari elaichi*)	2
Cinnamom (*dalchini*), 2" stick	1
Salt to taste	
Asafoetida (*hing*)	a pinch
Red chilli powder	2 tsp / 10 gm
Yoghurt (*dahi*)	2 tbsp / 30 gm
Water	1 cup / 200 ml
Ginger powder (*saunth*)	1 tsp / 5 gm
Aniseed (*saunf*) powder	1 tbsp / 15 gm
Garam masala (see p. 8)	1 tsp / 5 gm

Method:

1. Wash the kohlrabi, cut into ½"- thick rounds. Pierce all over with a fork and keep aside.
2. Heat the oil (for frying) in a pan. Fry the rounds to a golden brown. Put aside.
3. Heat 4 tbsp oil in a deep pot. Put in the cloves, bayleaves, black cardamoms, cinnamon, salt and asafoetida and lower the flame.
4. Add the red chilli powder mixed with yoghurt, stirring vigorously till the oil separates. Ensure that it does not stick to the bottom.
5. Add water, kohlrabi, ginger and aniseed powders and garam masala. Stir well and cook on a high flame until the gravy thickens and the oil separates. Serve hot.

Tchat Gogji
Mashed turnip

Preparation time: 10 min.
Cooking time: 20 min.
Serves: 4-6

Vegetarian

Ingredients:

Turnips (*shalgam*)	500 gm
Oil	3 tbsp / 45 ml
Asafoetida (*hing*)	a pinch
Sugar	a pinch
Salt to taste	
Whole red chillies (*sabut lal mirch*)	3
Tikki masala, crushed (see p. 8)	½ tsp / 3 gm
Water	½ cup / 100 ml

Method:

1. Wash and cut the turnips into thick, wafer-like slices.

2. Heat the oil in a heavy-bottomed pot. Add the turnips, asafoetida, sugar and salt to it.

3. Deseed the whole red chillies and break into two pieces. Add to the turnips and stir well. Cover the pot and cook over a high flame for 5 minutes.

4. Cook over a low flame, stirring often to make sure that the mixture doesn't stick to the bottom of the pot.

5. Add the *tikki masala*, along with water and stir well. Lightly mash the turnips with the back of the ladle, while stirring. Cook till the liquid almost dries up. Serve hot, accompanied by rice and plain yoghurt.

Monji Hak
Kohlrabi curry

Preparation time: 10 min.
Cooking time: 25 min.
Serves: 4-6

Ingredients:

Kohlrabi (*ganth gobhi*), with leaves   1 kg
Oil   3 tbsp / 45 ml
Asafoetida (*hing*)   a pinch
Salt to taste
Water   1 ½ cup / 300 ml
Whole red chillies (*sabut lal mirch*),
   deseeded   4
Tikki masala, crushed (see p. 8)   ½ tsp / 3 gm

(Photograph on page 2)

Method:

1. Separate the leaves of the kohlrabi and cut their stems. Peel the kohlrabi and slice into wafer-thin slices. Wash the leaves and slices well and put aside.
2. Heat the oil in a heavy-bottomed pot; add the kohlrabi, asafoetida and salt. Stir and then add the leaves. Cook for 2 minutes.
3. Add water and whole red chillies. Cook covered on a high flame for 10 minutes. Stir occasionally. Lower the flame and add the *tikki masala*. Stir well and cook uncovered over a low flame for 5-7 minutes. Tradionally the gravy is thin in consistency, but you can cook it to your preference.
4. Serve hot accompanied by boiled rice.

Nadur Monjivor
Lotus stems cutlets

Preparation time: 15 min.
Cooking time: 10 min.
Serves: 4-6

Ingredients:

Lotus stems (*bhein*)	250 gm
Arrowroot (*araroht*)	2 tbsp / 30 gm
Salt to taste	
Ginger (*adrak*), grated	2 tbsp / 30 gm
Red chilli powder (optional)	½ tsp / 3 gm
Oil for frying	½ cup / 100 ml

Method:

1. Scrape the lotus stems and cut the ends. Wash thoroughly under running water, ensuring that no mud remains in the stems.
2. Grate the lotus stems; mix with arrowroot, salt, ginger and red chilli powder.
3. Divide the mixture into six equal portions and shape each into flat round cutlets.
4. Heat the oil in a shallow pan. Carefully fry the cutlets a few at a time till they are golden brown on both sides. Serve hot.

Muji Meluvun
Mashed radish curry

Preparation time: 10 min.
Cooking time: 20 min.
Serves: 4-6

Vegetarian

Ingredients:

White radish (*safed mooli*), with leaves   1½ kg
Water   2½ cups / 500 ml
Oil   3 tbsp / 45 ml
Cloves (*laung*)   2
Whole red chillies (*sabut lal mirch*),
   deseeded   3-4
Ginger powder (*saunth*)   ½ tsp / 3 gm
Salt to taste
Asafoetida (*hing*)   a pinch
Tikki masala, crushed (see p. 8)   ½ tsp / 3 gm

Method:

1. Scrape and wash the radish. Remove the ends and dice. Separate the leaves and chop finely.
2. Heat the water in a heavy-bottomed pan. Put in the radish and the leaves. Cook for 10 minutes or until they get soft. Remove from the flame and drain the water.
3. Blend the boiled radish and leaves. Keep aside.
4. Heat the oil in a deep pan; add the cloves and the red chillies. Stir for a few seconds and then add the radish. Mix well and lower the flame.
5. Add the ginger powder, salt, asafoetida and the *tikki masala*. Cook covered for 5 minutes more. Serve hot with rice.

Barith Marchavangun
Stuffed green chillies

Preparation time: 20 min.
Cooking time: 10 min.
Serves: 4-6

Ingredients:

Green chillies, large	15-20
Vinegar (*sirka*)	½ cup / 100 ml
Walnuts (shelled)	¾ cup / 150 gm
Ginger (*adrak*), grated	2 tbsp / 30 gm
Pomegranate seeds (*anardana*)	3¼ tbsp / 50 gm
Cumin seeds (*jeera*)	1 tsp / 5 gm
Asafoetida (*hing*)	a pinch
Salt to taste	
Water	a few spoons
Oil for frying	½ cup / 100 ml

Method:

1. Wash the chillies and make a small slit in each. Deseed and soak them in vinegar for at least 1 hour.
2. Grind together to a smooth paste, the walnuts, ginger, pomegranate and cumin seeds, asafoetida and salt, adding a few spoons of water if necessary. Remove and keep in a small bowl.
3. Remove the chillies from the vinegar and spread out in a plate. Fill a little of the ground paste into the slits of the chillies. Do not overstuff, put only enough so as to allow the slits to remain closed. Keep them aside.
4. Heat the oil in a pan. Shallow fry the chillies over a low flame till they change colour (about a minute). Serve as a side dish.

Karela Yakhin
Bittergourd in yoghurt

Preparation time: 20 min.
Cooking time: 25 min.
Serves: 6-8

Vegetarian

Ingredients:

Bittergourds (*karela*), scraped, washed	1 kg
Oil for frying	1 cup / 200 ml
Oil	4 tbsp / 60 ml
Cloves (*laung*)	4
Green cardamoms (*choti elaichi*), crushed	4
Asafoetida (*hing*)	a pinch
Water	½ cup / 100 ml
Yoghurt (*dahi*), whisked	2 cups / 400 gm
Ginger powder (*saunth*)	1 tsp / 5 gm
Aniseed (*saunf*) powder	2 tsp / 10 gm
Garam masala (see p. 8)	1 tsp / 5 gm
Salt to taste	

Method:

1. Slit the bittergourds lengthwise on one side. Remove the seeds and spread the bittergourds on a plate. Rub 2 tsp of salt on them and put aside for 5 minutes. Wash well and drain excess water.
2. Heat the oil (for frying) and lightly fry the bittergourds on a high flame. Keep aside.
3. Heat 4 tbsp of oil in a pan; add the cloves, green cardamoms and asafoetida. Stir in the water and bring to a boil.
4. To the yoghurt, add ginger and aniseed powders, garam masala and salt. Add to the pan, stirring continuously, till the mixture boils.
5. Add the bittergourds. Cook till the gravy thickens and the oil separates. Serve hot.

Tud-Tud Bhata

Fried rice

Preparation time: 5 min.
Cooking time: 15 min.
Serves: 2-4

Ingredients:

Cooked rice	3 cups
Oil	3 tbsp / 45 ml
Cumin seeds (*jeera*)	½ tsp / 3 gm
Cloves (*laung*)	3
Red chilli powder	½ tsp / 3 gm
Water	3 tbsp / 45 ml
Salt to taste	
Ginger powder (*saunth*)	½ tsp / 3 gm
Eggs (optional)	4

Method:

1. Heat the oil in a deep pan. Add the cumin seeds and cloves; sauté for a few seconds.
2. Mix the red chilli powder in a few spoons of water and add to the pan. Stir, and then quickly add the cooked rice.
3. Mix well and cook over a slow flame. Mix in the salt and ginger powder. When the rice is heated through, transfer to a serving dish.
4. Fry the eggs and then garnish the rice with them. Serve hot.

Kanguchi Pulao
Mushroom pulao

Preparation time: 10 min.
Cooking time: 30 min.
Serves: 4-6

Ingredients:

Rice, washed, soaked in water	1½ cups/300 gm
Black mushrooms (*guchchi*)	100 gm
Clarified butter (*ghee*)	5 tbsp / 75 gm
Cloves (*laung*)	6
Black cardamoms (*bari elaichi*), crushed	4
Green cardamoms (*choti elaichi*)	6
Cinnamon (*dalchini*), 1" sticks	3
Bayleaves (*tej patta*)	3
Almonds (*badaam*), blanched	75 gm
Asafoetida (*hing*)	a pinch
Salt to taste	
Water	5 cups / 1 lt
Ginger powder (*saunth*)	1 tsp / 5 gm
Saffron (*kesar*)	2 pinches
Garam masala (see p. 8)	1 tsp / 5 gm

Method:

1. Slit the mushrooms lengthwise and wash well.
2. Heat the clarified butter in a heavy-bottomed pot. Add cloves, black and green cardamoms, cinnamon sticks, bayleaves and almonds. Stir for a few seconds, then add the mushrooms.
3. Add asafoetida and salt; sauté for 1 minute, and then add the rice (drained). Stir gently, add 3 cups of water and bring to a boil. Add ginger powder.
4. Mix the saffron in 2 tsp of hot water and crush with a spoon. Add to rice, cook covered for 15 minutes.
5. When the water is almost absorbed, transfer the pot over an electric hot plate or a griddle (*tawa*) over a low flame. Cook covered, till the rice is done. Sprinkle garam masala before serving.

Ninya Pulao
Lamb pulao

Preparation time: 10 min.
Cooking time: 45 min.
Serves: 6-8

Ingredients:

Rice, washed, soaked, drained	3 cups / 600 gm
Water	10 cups / 2 lt
Lamb	750 gm
Ginger powder (*saunth*)	1 tsp / 5 gm
Aniseed (*saunf*) powder	2 tsp / 10 gm
Asafoetida (*hing*)	a pinch
Salt to taste	
Clarified butter (*ghee*)	6 tbsp / 90 gm
Cloves (*laung*)	6
Black cardamoms (*bari elaichi*), crushed	4
Green cardamoms (*choti elaichi*), crushed	6
Cinnamon (*dalchini*), 1" sticks	3
Bayleaves (*tej patta*)	3
Almonds (*badam*), blanched	½ cup / 100 gm
Saffron (*kesar*)	2 pinches
Garam masala (see p. 8)	1 tsp / 5 gm

Method:

1. Heat 5 cups of water. Add the lamb, ginger and aniseed powders, asafoetida and salt. Cook covered on a high flame until the lamb is almost done. Separate the lamb from the stock. Put both aside.
2. Heat the clarified butter in a deep pot; add all the ingredients from cloves to almonds, and the lamb. Sauté for a minute, add the rice and sauté further for 1 minute. Add 6 cups of stock (adding water if needed) and stir gently.
3. Mix saffron with a little hot water and grind. Add to the pot, cook covered on a high flame until the water is almost absorbed. Place the pot over a griddle (*tawa*), cook covered over a low flame, till the rice is done. Sprinkle garam masala and serve.

Bazabata
Mixed vegetable rice

Preparation time: 15 min.
Cooking time: 30 min.
Serves: 2-4

Ingredients:

Rice	1½ cups / 300 gm
Clarified butter (*ghee*)	4 tbsp / 60 gm
Cloves (*laung*)	4
Black cardamoms (*bari elaichi*), crushed	2
Cauliflower (*phool gobi*), cut into florets	500 gm
Potatoes, peeled, cut into 4 pieces	250 gm
Peas (*mattar*), shelled	1¼ cups / 250 gm
Asafoetida (*hing*)	a pinch
Salt to taste	
Turmeric (*haldi*) powder	1 tsp / 5 gm
Water	3 cups / 600 ml
Ginger powder (*saunth*)	1 tsp / 5 gm
Green chillies, slit	2
Ginger (*adrak*), fresh, ½" piece, julienned	1

Method:

1. Pick, clean and wash the rice. Keep aside.
2. Heat the oil in a heavy-bottomed pot. Add the cloves and black cardamoms and stir. Add all the vegetables, asafoetida, salt and turmeric powder. Stir for one minute.
3. Add the rice and stir again. Add the water, ginger powder, green chillies and ginger. Cover and cook for 20 minutes, stirring occasionally.
4. When the water is almost absorbed, transfer the pot over a electric hot plate or a griddle, over a low flame. Cook covered on a low flame for 5-7 minutes. Serve with yoghurt, pickle or chutney.

Tamatar Chetin
Tomato chutney

Preparation time: 20 min.
Cooking time: 1 hr.
Serves: 4-6

Ingredients:

Tomatoes	2 kg
Water, boiling hot	15 cups / 3 lt
Sugar	2½ cups / 500 gm
Vinegar (*sirka*)	1½ cup / 300 ml
Salt	5 tsp / 25 gm
Red chilli powder	2 tbsp / 30 gm
Ginger powder (*saunth*)	1 tbsp / 15 gm
Garam masala (see p. 8)	1 tbsp / 15 gm
Ginger (*adrak*), chopped	5 tsp / 25 gm
Raisins (*kishmish*), soaked in water	½ cup / 100 gm

Method:

1. Immerse the tomatoes in the boiling water. Cover with a lid and let them stand in hot water for 15 minutes. Remove and dry carefully with a cloth.
2. Peel and mash them to pulp. Add sugar, salt, red chilli powder, ginger powder and vinegar; cook till the mixture comes to a boil.
3. Add the garam masala, ginger and raisins. Cook on a slow fire, till sufficiently thick. Remove from the fire, cool and bottle.

*(Photograph on page 79, **top:** Tamatar Chetin; **bottom left:** Pudna Chetin; **bottom right:** Doon Chetin.)*

Doon Chetin
Walnut chutney

Preparation time: 15 min. Serves: 8-10

Ingredients:

Walnuts (*akhroth*), without shells	½ cup / 100 gm
Onions, chopped	½ cup / 100 gm
Green chillies, chopped	2
Yoghurt (*dahi*)	½ cup / 100 gm
Red chilli powder	¼ tsp / 1½ gm
Salt to taste	

Method:

1. Grind together the onions and green chillies to a smooth paste. Add the walnuts and grind further for 30-40 seconds.
2. Transfer the mixture to a bowl. Mix in the yoghurt, red chilli powder, salt and serve.

Pudna Chetin
Mint chutney

Preparation time: 20 min. Serves: 8-10

Ingredients:

Mint (*pudina*) leaves, washed	150 gm
Green chillies, chopped	2-3
Water	2 tsp / 10 ml
Yoghurt (*dahi*), whisked	2 tbsp / 30 gm
Salt to taste	

Method:

1. Put the mint and chillies into a grinder with the water and grind to a smooth paste. Transfer to a small bowl.
2. Mix the yoghurt into the mint leave paste. Add the salt to taste and serve.

Marchavangan Chetin
Green chilli chutney

Preparation time: 15 min. Serves: 4-6

Ingredients:

Green chillies, diced	½ cup / 100 gm
Salt to taste	
Water	2 tsp / 10 ml
Yoghurt (*dahi*); optional	1 tsp / 15 gm

Method:

1. Grind the chillies with salt and water into a coarse paste. Remove the lid of the grinder carefully or your eyes will sting.
2. Add the yoghurt to this paste and serve.

Muji Chetin
Radish chutney

Preparation time: 20 min. Serves: 4-6

Ingredients:

Radish (*mooli*), scraped, grated	¾ cup / 150 gm
Yoghurt (*dahi*), whisked	1 cup / 200 gm
Salt to taste	
Red chilli powder	½ tsp / 3 gm

Method:

1. Squeeze the radish with both your hands and then put it in the serving bowl.
2. Mix the yoghurt into the radish, add salt and red chilli powder and serve.

*(**Left:** Marchavangan Chetin; **right:** Muji Chetin)* ▶

Accompaniments

Monji Anchaar
Kohlrabi pickle

Preparation time: 30 min.
Serves: 2-4

I n g r e d i e n t s :

Kohlrabi (*ganth gobhi*), only bulbs	1 kg
Mustard (*sarson*) oil	1¼ cup / 250 ml
Red chilli powder	3 tbsp / 45 gm
Ginger powder (*saunth*)	2 tsp / 10 gm
Asafoetida (*hing*)	¼ tsp / 1¼ gm
Mustard seeds (*rai*)	45 gm / 3 tbsp
Carom seeds (*ajwain*)	5 gm / 1 tsp
Salt to taste	

M e t h o d :

1. Wash the kohlrabi. Dry with a soft cloth and cut the bulb into half. Make ⅓"-thick slices, without peeling. Dry these slices in the sun for 3-4 hours.

2. Heat half the oil, cool and then put aside. In the remaining oil, mix all the spices well with hand.

3. Add the slices of kohlrabi. Mix well so that the slices are well coated with the paste.

4. Take a large dry jar and put the spiced slices and any extra oil in the pot, in it. Seal with a polyfilm and then put on the lid.

5. Keep this jar in the sun for 4-6 days (in winter) and 2-3 days (in summer). At first the level of oil will rise in the jar and will then settle down.

6. When the oil settles down, pour the remaining oil into it so that the kohlrabi slices are covered with oil.

7. Keep in the sun for a few more days.

Muji Talai
Fried radish chutney

Preparation time: 10 min.
Cooking time: 20 min.
Serves: 6-8

Ingredients:

White radish (*safed mooli*), grated	2½ cups / 500 gm
Oil	4 tbsp / 60 ml
Carom (*ajwain*) seeds	½ tsp / 3 gm
Cumin seeds (*jeera*)	½ tsp / 3 gm
Salt to taste	
Asafoetida (*hing*)	a pinch
Turmeric (*haldi*) powder	½ tsp / 3 gm
Ginger powder (*saunth*)	½ tsp / 3 gm
Aniseed (*saunf*) powder	½ tsp / 3 gm
Red chilli powder (optional)	½ tsp / 3 gm
Green chilli, chopped	1
Juice of lemon (*nimbu*)	1
Walnuts (*akhrot*), crushed	¼ cup / 50 gm

Method:

1. Heat the oil in a pan; add carom seeds, cumin seeds, salt and asafoetida.
2. Stir for 30 seconds, then add the radish. Cook over a medium flame till the water evaporates and the oil separates.
3. Add turmeric, ginger, aniseed and red chilli powders, the green chilli and lemon juice.
4. Cook for about 5 minutes, then add the walnuts.

Modur Pulao

Sweetened rice

Preparation time: 15 min.
Cooking time: 30 min.
Serves: 4-6

Desserts

Ingredients:

Basmati rice, washed, soaked for 1 hr	300 gm
Milk	5 cups / 1 lt
Sugar	2 cups / 400 gm
Saffron (*kesar*)	2 gm
Clarified butter (*ghee*)	5 tbsp / 75 gm
Almonds (*badam*)	½ cup / 100 gm
Cashewnut (*kaju*)	¼ cup / 50 gm
Currants (*kishmish*)	¼ cup / 50 gm
Coconut (*nariyal*), diced	¼ cup / 50 gm
Cinnamon (*dalchini*), 1" sticks	3
Green cardamoms (*choti elaichi*)	6
Black peppercorns (*sabut kali mirch*)	6
Bayleaves (*tej patta*)	2
Cloves (*laung*)	6

Method:

1. Heat the milk in a heavy-bottomed pot. Add the rice (drained) and cook on a low flame till the milk begins to get absorbed. Remove from the flame, keeping the rice a little under done.
2. Transfer the rice to a large flat dish. Add the sugar and mix well gently.
3. Soak the saffron in ¼ cup hot water for 5 minutes.
4. Heat the clarified butter in a heavy-bottomed pot. Lightly fry the dry fruits and coconut, cinnamon, green cardamoms, peppercorns and bayleaves.
5. Add the rice and the saffron water. Stir well, gently.
6. Put a flat pan/griddle under the pot and cook covered, over a low flame till done. Garnish with cloves and serve hot.

Shufta
Dry fruits in sugar syrup

Preparation time: 20 min.
Cooking time: 15 min.
Serves: 10-15

Ingredients:

Cottage cheese (*paneer*), ½'' cubes	250 gm
Clarified butter (*ghee*) for frying	
Clarified butter (*ghee*)	2 tbsp / 30 gm
Almonds (*badam*), blanched	½ cup / 100 gm
Currants (*kishmish*),	½ cup / 100 gm
Coconut (*nariyal*), slivered	¼ cup / 50 gm
Dried dates (*khajoor*), deseeded, slivered	¼ cup / 50 gm
Black peppercorns (*sabut kali mirch*)	1 tsp / 5 gm
Water	1 cup / 200 ml
Sugar	1½ cup / 300 gm
Green cardamoms (*choti elaichi*), crushed	6
Saffron (*kesar*)	½ tsp / 3 gm
Candied sugar (*misri*)	¼ cup / 50 gm
Lemon (*nimbu*) juice	1 tbsp / 15 ml

Method:

1. Heat the clarified butter (for frying) and fry the cottage cheese lightly. Remove and put aside.
2. Heat 30 gm of clarified butter in a pot. Lightly sauté the almonds, currants, coconut, dates and peppercorns for 1 minute.
3. Add water, sugar and green cardamoms. Stir till the water comes to a boil. Lower the flame and cook for 5 minutes.
4. Soak the saffron in 2 tsp of hot water and crush it with the back of a spoon. Mix into the pot and stir well.
5. Add the candied sugar and the lemon juice; stir again. When the syrup becomes thick (not dry), remove from the flame. Serve warm.

Phirun
Rice pudding

Preparation time: 15 min.
Cooking time: 40 min.
Serves: 6-8

Ingredients:

Rice	¾ cup / 150 gm
Milk	5 cups / 1 lt
Green cardamoms (*choti elaichi*), crushed	4
Almonds (*badam*), blanched, slivered	3 ¼ tbsp / 50 gm
Saffron (*kesar*)	a pinch
Sugar	1¼ cups / 250 gm
Silver leaves (*chandi vark*)	8
Clay bowls (*kasore*), soaked in water	8

Method:

1. Pick, clean and wash the rice. Soak it in water for 3-4 hours. Drain the water and let the rice dry. When dry, either crumble it or grind coarsely for 10 seconds.

2. Heat the milk in a heavy-bottomed pot. Bring to a boil, add the rice, green cardamoms and almonds to it. Stir frequently with a ladle.

3. Lower the flame and cook till the rice gets soft and the milk thickens. Stir frequently to ensure that it doesn't stick to the bottom.

4. Crush the saffron and soak in a few spoons of hot milk. Add to the pot, followed by the sugar. Stir for a few minutes and remove from the flame.

5. Remove the clay bowls from the water, and allow them to dry. When the *phirun* is ready, ladle it out into separate bowls. Decorate with silver leaves and serve chilled.

Suggested Menus

Non-vegetarian

Kokur Nadur (*Chicken with lotus stems*) 29
Kashur Gaad (*Tamarind-flavoured fish curry*) 32
Kabargah (*Fried ribs*) 16

or

Vegetarian

Chaman Olu (*Cottage cheese and potatoes*) 44
Hak (*Stir-fried spinach*) 56

Accompaniments

Tud-Tud Bhata (*Fried rice*) 70
Doon Chetin (*Walnut chutney*) 78
Monji Achaar (*Kohlrabi pickle*) 82

Dessert

Shufta (*Dry fruits in sugar syrup*) 88

Non-vegetarian

Kokur Roganjosh (*Chicken curry*) 30
Thool Zamboor (*Fried egg curry*) 34
Yakhni (*Stewed lamb in yoghurt*) 24

or

Vegetarian

Monji Kalia (*Kohlrabi stew*) 46
Tsok Vangun (*Tangy brinjals*) 54

Accompaniments

Ninya Pulao (*Lamb pulao*) 74
Muji Chetin (*Radish chutney*) 80

Desserts

Phirun (*Rice pudding*) 90

Glossary of Cooking Terms

Blanch — Immerse in boiling water so that the peel comes off.

Dice — Cut into small cubes.

Fillet — The undercut of a loin or ribs of meat, boned sides of fish or boned breasts of poultry.

Marinate — The process in which a product (meat, fish or vegetable) is steeped in a mixture of seasoning ingredients, to add flavour to the product and to make it tender.

Sauté — Fry quickly over strong heat in oil or clarified butter.

Simmer — Cook gently over a low flame.

Stir-fry — Fry rapidly while stirring and tossing.

Temper — Combine spices and flavourings with hot oil/clarified butter, and then pour this over the main preparation.

Whisk — To beat air rapidly into a mixture with an egg beater, rotary beater or an electric beater.

Index

ISBN: 81-7436-117-0

Second impression 2003
© **Roli & Janssen BV 2000**
Published in India by Roli Books
in arrangement with Roli & Janssen BV
M 75, Greater Kailash II Market, New Delhi-110 048, India
Tel.: ++91 (011) 26442271, 26462782; Fax: ++91 (011) 26467185
E-mail: roli@vsnl.com; Website: rolibooks.com

Photographs: Dheeraj Paul

Printed and bound in Singapore